Also by Donald G. Southerton

Non-fiction

The Filleys: 350 Years of American Entrepreneurial Spirit

Intrepid Americans: Bold Koreans—Early Korean Trade, Concessions, and Entrepreneurship

The Sioux in South Dakota (Contributing author)

Chemulpo to Songdo IBD: Korea's International Gateway

Fiction

A Yankee in the Land of the Morning Calm: A Historical Novel Book One, 1890-1895

A Yankee in the Land of the Morning Calm: Gold and Rail Book Two, 1895-1900

A Yankee in the Land of the Morning Calm: The Northern Frontier Book Three, 1900-1907

eBooks

Coffee, Cars, and Corporations: Thoughts on Korean Business and Popular Culture

More Thoughts on Korean Business and Popular Culture: Volume 2

Hyundai and Kia Motors—The Early Years and Product Development

Colorado's Henry Collbran and the Roots of Early Korean Entrepreneurialism

Korea Facing: Secrets for Success in Korean Global Business

Hyundai Way

Hyundai Speed

Donald G. Southerton

Copyright © 2014

By

Donald G. Southerton

All rights reserved.

10 9 8 7 6

Library of Congress Cataloging-in-Publication Data

Southerton, Donald G. 1953-

Contents

Acknowledgements

Foreword

Disclaimer

Introduction
The Quest
A Shared Mindset
Corporate Culture—Art or Science
A Starting Point: Entrepreneurship
Global Success
Chapter Overviews

Chapter 1

Korea and Its Culture
Dynamic Korea
Korean Entrepreneurship
Confucianism

Chapter 2

Hyundai Heritage
Chung Ju-yung—Hyundai Founder and Honorary Chairman
The Early Years
Hyundai and the "Miracle on the Han"
Empire
Nation-Builder to Philanthropy

Transition and Family Succession

Chairman Chung Mong Koo

110 Days

The Pony

The 1990s

Record Sales

Impact of the IMF Crisis

Turning Point

Chapter 3

A Unique Corporate Culture, Old and New

Sahoon

Together For A Better Future

Linking the Past, Present and Future

Chapter 4

Management Styles

The Role of Mentoring

Globality

A Growing Trend

Conclusions

My concerns regarding sustainability

In Conclusion

About the Author

Credits

Endnotes

Acknowledgements

This book's content is built upon considerable historical and contemporary research. In crafting this work, I have benefited enormously from many people and resources. My first thanks must go to the Hyundai Motor organization for allowing me the opportunity to experience and share their culture and accomplishments.

In particular, I owe a special thanks to my friends at Hyundai Motor, Kia Motors, Hyundai MOBIS, Innocean Media Worldwide, Hyundai GLOVIS, Hyundai Capital, and sister companies. This book would not be possible without their strong support.

Finally, Diana Southerton Rudloff and Anna Cash-Mitchell have truly been partners in this work from concept to the final copy. I deeply appreciate Diana's meticulous proofing of the manuscript, probing comments, and numerous editorial suggestions. Equally valued are Anna's creative skills and technical savvy in the layout of both in the eBook and print formats. Their assistance throughout the project merits very special thanks.

Foreword

HYUNDAI
MOTOR GROUP

The Hyundai name and brand have steadily gained global recognition. Established in the late 1940s, Hyundai's growth over the next decades paralleled South Korea's rise as an emerging and vigorous economy. By the early 2000s the highly diversified Hyundai Group restructured and split into a number of independent and specialized units, including Hyundai Heavy Industries (HHI), Hyundai Merchant Marine (HMM), Hyundai Engineering and Construction (HEC), and Hyundai Motor Company (HMC). As Hyundai Motor expanded into a highly integrated auto manufacturer composed of numerous sister companies and subsidiaries, the name, too, evolved. By 2011, with the latter company surpassing the original organization and former affiliates in overall global success, it was renamed the Hyundai Motor Group with focus on three growth engines—automotive, steel, and construction

To avoid confusion, I use Hyundai Motor Group when discussing the mother organization and terms like Hyundai Motor Company (HMC) and Kia Motors Company (KMC) when referring to specific divisions. That said, at times I use "Hyundai" and "Hyundai Motor" in a broad inclusive sense with regard to culture and heritage.

Disclaimer

To clarify, this book shares no trade secrets, but looks to provide insights into Hyundai's corporate culture. The viewpoints presented in the book are that solely of the author.

Introduction

The Quest

Hyundai has a rich heritage, a history of overcoming great challenges, and a legacy of bold innovations and positive, forward thinking. *"So, what makes Hyundai so successful?"* In the wake of Hyundai's recent accomplishments this is a question often raised, but rarely answered. An objective of *Hyundai Way: Hyundai Speed* is to convey insights into the Hyundai Motor Group—a unique inside view of a unique corporate culture—as well as to share my quest to uncover, define, and communicate the true *Hyundai Way*.

Stepping back to August 2005, I was conducting cross-cultural training and coaching sessions at Hyundai Motor's newest manufacturing facility in Montgomery, Alabama. In the early months of the car plant operations, tensions between the American and Korean teams were mounting. Production of the first vehicles in a new facility is always a daunting task. The additional cultural dimensions and language differences only compounded the odds of having a smooth launch. Recognizing the challenges, senior Korean leadership asked if I could provide team-building workshops that would allow managers to better address escalating concerns and issues.

Consensus was that the problem was "cultural"—Koreans not understanding Americans and visa-versa. I had been working across the Hyundai and Kia Motors organization for several years and I had dealt with what I thought were similar situations. However, a few hours into the Alabama workshops I uncovered the true cause of the strained relationship, but it was not what I had expected.

Most of the American teams were veterans of car manufacturing—hand picked because they had been top performers at Ford, Toyota, Nissan, Honda, Mercedes Benz, and GM North American plants. In contrast, the Korean teams were Hyundai Motor Company career employees—most having worked for a decade or more at Alabama's sister plant in Asan, South Korea.

What surfaced in discussions was that many of the new American managers had been searching in earnest for a *Hyundai Way*—documented policies and procedures that would guide them in decision-making and day-to-day work. For example, former Toyota managers looked for a model similar to the *Toyota Way*, while others who had worked for Ford Motor Company sought standard operation procedures (SOPs). Not finding a set *Hyundai Way* resulted in some Americans feeling that there might be a communications and language issue. More concerning, a few hinted strongly at trust issues and that Koreans were deliberately withholding vital information.

Listening to the group, I had a realization. Over the years working with Hyundai and other Korea-based businesses, I found sharing historic background and differences between Korean culture and other cultures as a proven, effective and commonly accepted cross-cultural learning model. Nevertheless, it became crystal clear to me that what was truly needed in this situation was to clarify and impart an intangible—the *Hyundai Way* or vision. The problem was that a true grasp of HMC goes beyond in-house corporate value training programs produced by human resources and organizational development teams. PowerPoint presentations and manuals are not sufficient. Instead, understanding a corporate culture is experiential, situational, and acquired over time.

A Shared Mindset

Jumping forward several years... on a number of occasions, and triggered by the work in Alabama, I have shared my quest to better understand the *Hyundai Way* with veteran Korean staff and executives. Time and time again, I found those long employed by the Company reflecting for a moment and then stating frankly that the Hyundai approach was not easy to explain. For example, one senior Korean pointed out that within Hyundai there are several management styles and approaches to tackling an issue depending on the person's *lineage*. Groomed by their seniors, junior members of teams adopt the mentor's methodology and leadership style—some "hard" and demanding, others "soft" and preferring collaboration.

Another Hyundai executive imparted that the *Hyundai Way* was acquired over time. He added that, with the exception of some minor differences among the sister companies, the transferring of key people among the companies, such as Hyundai Motor, Kia Motors, and Hyundai Mobis (the parts and modular division), creates a shared mindset. At a minimum, Korean teams understand the thought process and methods of others across the organization regardless of the affiliations.

The Korean executives did agree that understanding the corporate mindset by both Koreans and non-Koreans working across the organization was vital to the continued success of the Company. My quest has been an ongoing pursuit to define and share that mindset.

Corporate Culture—Art or Science

Defining intangibles, such as a company's culture, heritage, and core values, is a challenge. Like fish in water, we often fail to "see" our culture and values because they are the mediums within which we work and exist. In addition, even when clearly defined, transferring corporate intangibles across cultural and regional borders is difficult. That said, top global companies do, in fact, recognize the need and find ways to share these intangibles with their teams and organizations.

Building on the strong vision for the organization of the late Hyundai founder Chung Ju Yung, we also recognize the powerful influence his son Chairman Chung Mong Koo has had on the firm's culture. As of this writing the *Hyundai Way* continues to evolve with the third generation, Vice-Chairman Chung Eui-sun now assuming a key leadership position at HMC.

A Starting Point: Entrepreneurship

In the course of crafting this work, a driving force that continually surfaced was Korean entrepreneurship. Exploring the strong ties between entrepreneurship and Hyundai culture is then a second goal for this book. However, economists accept no single definition of entrepreneurship or one that fits all economies and eras. For example, Alfred Marshall in his 1890 classic *Principles of Economics* noted that entrepreneurs were the driving force behind industry, act with limited information, and that entrepreneurship was a rare skill.[i] In contrast, noted economist Harvey Leibenstein argues that the dominant characteristic of entrepreneurs is their ability to perceive gaps in markets. They then develop new goods, services, or processes to fit those needs. Moreover, Leibenstein points out that entrepreneurs have the ability to innovatively combine various inputs to satisfy the market. [ii] In turn, esteemed management guru Peter Drucker in *Innovation and Entrepreneurship: Practice and Principles* found that in some cases, entrepreneurs may not produce a new product but use creative innovation to apply knowledge and technology developed elsewhere to their local market niche. [iii]

By combining relevant theories I have arrived at a generalized set of qualities which aptly apply to Hyundai as discussed in this work. Hyundai leadership has a long history as risk takers, organizers, coordinators, gap-fillers, and innovators. They seek out new ways of approaching a challenge, benchmark against top competitors, and quickly implement new practices.

Global Success

A final goal of this book is to share Hyundai's global success model—including the challenges of running a highly integrated manufacturing organization with operations worldwide. These challenges are compounded with the Group's growth initiative of expanding beyond autos to fully integrate steel and construction within the Hyundai Motor Group family. I also provide some thoughts on prospects for the brand's continued, sustained growth.

Chapter Overviews

"Chapter 1 Korea and its Culture" will explore the ties between Korean and Hyundai heritage with deeply rooted culture and tradition still strongly impacting the modern workplace.

After sharing this background on Korea, "Chapter 2 Hyundai Heritage" will look at the rise of Hyundai under its founder Chung Ju Yung (1915-2001). With changing times, by the late 1990s, Hyundai Motors would witness a new era of leadership and renewed direction under the founder's son Chung Mong Koo. Most significant was the new chairman's hands-on approach to management and issues including quality and global expansion.

Next, "Chapter 3 A Unique Corporate Culture" will focus on Hyundai corporate culture, old and new—values that link Hyundai heritage, the Founder Chung Ju Yung, and current chairman Chung Mong Koo. Then, in "Chapter 4" we look at the *Hyundai Way* through notable company management styles. If you recall from earlier in this Introduction, I noted that there are a number of Hyundai management styles. Those working with Korean teams from Hyundai, Kia, MOBIS, and the affiliates will quickly recognize these methods and practices—once they are pointed out!

"Conclusions", the final chapter of *Hyundai Way: Hyundai Speed*, shares the author's opinions on a question so many have asked of this enigmatic system: "Is Hyundai business model globally sustainable?" I tackle this question from the cultural perspective.

Chapter 1

Korea and Its Culture

It is not surprising that many Korean firms, Hyundai included, draw upon inherent ethnic strengths and talents. Although diverse and global organizations, at the core they are very Korean in their mindsets and practices. Culture does play a strong role. The same could be said for Italian Gucci, German Bosch, Japanese Honda or America's Apple and Starbucks. Chapter 1 begins by providing background on Korea, its people, and how during the last decades of the twentieth century the nation modernized. In particular I will discuss how Hyundai has incorporated traditions and values that not only supported their early development but also contribute to present day successes.

Dynamic Korea

Koreans share a rich heritage, a prospering economy, and a vibrant society. We will first look at some interesting background on Korea: past and present.

Land and History: Korea is located in northeast Asia. Its neighbors include China, Japan, and Russia. South Korea has a land area of 98,500 sq. km. (38,000 sq. mi.) with a population around 50 million people. In terms of size the combined landmass of North and South Korea is similar to the state of Utah, with South Korea about the size of Indiana or Kentucky.

East Asia

Geography: Korea is a diverse land of scenic coastlines, rolling hills, rugged mountains, and picturesque valleys. With a temperate climate, Koreans experience four distinct seasons. Spring and autumn are rather short, summer is hot and humid, and winter is cold and dry with occasional snowfall, especially in the mountainous regions. The autumn season also finds various folk festivals rooted in ancient agrarian customs.

People: Reaching back to the Neolithic Period before 6000 BC, inhabitants on the peninsula have been a distinct endogamous ethnic group. Clan-based communities that formed walled towns and villages characterized ancient Korea. By the first century BC an era of confederated kingdoms emerged, eventually unifying the peninsula by 688 AD. Over the next 1300 years Korea maintained its identity even against a Manchu invasion in 1627, a series of Japanese invasions from 1592 to 1598 and the Japanese colonial rule and annexation (1904-1945).

Tradition: Reaching back centuries, traditional Korean music, architecture, cuisine, and clothing are unique to the country and although they share similarities with their East Asian neighbors Japan and China, there are differences, for example, in language and foods like *kimchi*. Philosophically, Korean tradition is rooted in Confucianism and manifested in a calm but dynamic and disciplined approach to life.

Despite modernization and globalization, this distinct culture still thrives and has a powerful effect on contemporary Korea; we find these traditional influences shaping modern design and architecture. Other aspects of this traditional mindset can be seen in Koreans' strong emphasis on education. In the workplace, norms and customs rooted in Korean tradition include respect for seniors and an emphasis on group harmony and teamwork.

Achievements as a Nation: During the last decades, South Korea has become a global leader of industrial innovation. For example, Korea is the world's largest shipbuilding nation. In addition, Korea controls a sizable global market share in the semiconductor sector, in particular in digital flash memory and Dynamic Random Access Memory. Other top sectors of industrial innovation include consumer electronics, such as smartphones and home appliances. In more recent years, South Korea has emerged as the one of the world's largest car manufacturer boosted by Hyundai Motor's and sister company Kia Motors' contributions. Similar to Korea's society, the country's economy is vibrant and trend setting.

Modern Korea: With bright lights, high tech buildings, world-class fashions, and a fast pace, Korea is an evolving society embracing the future. Predominately urban, nearly half the population lives near Seoul, one of the largest cities in the world. Seoul hosted the Olympics in 1988 and the opening of the World Cup in 2002. In 2010, Seoul was designated a World Design Capital, joining the ranks of Paris and Milan as a globally recognized center of design. [iv] Looking forward, South Korea will host the XXIII Winter Olympics in 2018.

Korean Entrepreneurship

In a 1996 interview management guru Peter Drucker pointed out that the South Koreans are among the top entrepreneurial people in the world. [v] Drucker noted that the setbacks of the Japanese Colonial Period, the post-World War II split of the country, and the Korean War were obstacles to Korea's development; however, Koreans must possess inherent tendencies towards innovation and entrepreneurialism in order to have gained so much in recent decades. Related to this, contemporary western economists find multiple reasons for South

Korea's economic success. Among the explanations are government policies, a well-educated and disciplined work force, the *dae kieop* (large-scale business) model, and the relentless drive of the family-run conglomerate founders. [vi]

Confucianism

An additional strength recognized by observers today is Korean Neo-Confucian culture—the peninsula's dominate social-political force for over six centuries. Neo-Confucian culture's respect for authority, emphasis on education, loyalty to the family and harmony within the group are often cited as key elements in post-Korean War South Korea's economic rise. [vii] Korean Neo-Confucian pro-education leanings created a ready workforce adept at learning modern technology at both the operational and management levels. [viii]

Another Confucian value, loyalty to the family and group, has allowed Koreans today, as in the past, to align themselves toward achieving a collective task vital to industrial society and productivity.[ix] Together with the Korean Neo-Confucian importance of *inhwa* (harmony), we find a large workforce well suited to tasks requiring cooperation and team-effort.

In conclusion, Hyundai is a very modern company but the role of Korean culture still strongly impacts day-to-day operation of the Group and its subsidiaries and cannot be under estimated. Culture matters. This then raises a question, "As Hyundai continues to move into new markets, will the company retain its 'Korean-ness' and will Hyundai also become adept at assimilating other cultures to succeed and mold the *Hyundai Way* as needed?"

Chapter 2

Hyundai Heritage

A company's initial culture is usually determined by its founder's mindset—the person's values, beliefs, preferences... Jim C. Collins, author Built to Last *and* Good to Great

Chung Ju-yung—Hyundai Founder and Honorary Chairman

Growing up in rural Korea during the Japanese Colonial era, the future founder of Hyundai, Chung Ju-yung, exhibited entrepreneurialism early in life. Breaking free from Korean agrarian tradition that the eldest son remain at home to tend the family lands, young Chung's desire to enter business led to his operating a rice store and then an auto repair business while still a young man. Following the liberation of Korea from Japan in 1945 and unshackled by draconian Colonial rule, Chung Ju-yung re-entered the auto repair business and soon after formed a construction company. He named these businesses *Hyundai*, which means *Modern*.

The Early Years

After several years of prosperity and capitalizing on expansion opportunities, Chung Ju-yung was suddenly forced to abandon the Seoul-based auto repair and construction companies in 1950 when North Korea invaded South Korea. Along with thousand of other refugees, Chung Ju-yung and his extended family fled to the last bastion of resistance, the southern coastal city of Busan. There an opportunity to provide housing for the American military surfaced and soon Chung Ju-yung was back in business as a contractor. No construction job was turned away—big or small.

In the years following the end of the Korean War in 1953, Chung Ju-yung and Hyundai established themselves as a reputable construction company. Working mostly for the Americans and the South Korean government, Hyundai struggled with extremely limited resources to restore Korea's war-battered infrastructure. A key project drawing considerable public attention was the rebuilding of Seoul's single bridge spanning the Han River. To thwart the advancing North Korean army, the bridge had been destroyed by the South Koreans on the third day of the Korean War. In the spirit of nationalism, Chung Ju-yung repaired the bridge "at cost." This drew strong local accolades, while establishing the previously little known Hyundai as a major Korean construction company in the eyes of the public and the government.

Hyundai and the "Miracle on the Han"

Fueled by a wide spread perception of post-war government mismanagement and corruption, in 1961 South Korea witnessed a military coup led by General Park Chung-Hee. In the wake of the coup as South Korea struggled to recover from the devastation of the conflict and an ever present and looming threat from North Korea, the new regime saw the need for rapid social and economic development. To spur this rapid economic development the authoritarian South Korean government teamed with a number of the Korean family-run businesses commonly referred to as *chaebol (chae=* wealth, *bol* = family*)*. The new regime managed in a *quid pro quo* relationship, providing the *chaebol* with subsidies, cheap credit and protection against foreign competition. This arrangement also limited Unions, which kept labor cost low. Korean *chaebol* that met the authoritarian government's bold mandates gained additional work. In a climate where failure was not tolerated and success rewarded, Hyundai was among the most successful. Moreover, Chung Ju-yung gained a reputation for iron-will, determination, and a "can-do" spirit where "even the impossible was possible."

By the 1970s and 1980s, the South Korean economy began to focus on export-driven heavy industry. Chung Ju-yung continued to diversify the company by entering key sectors, including shipbuilding and auto manufacturing. In many cases, Hyundai divisions were the preferred suppliers to others within the Group—ranging from concrete to steel. By the 1980s, Hyundai was South Korea's largest and most successful conglomerate with projects across Asia and the Middle East. To many Hyundai symbolized South Korea's rapid economic growth often referred to as the "Miracle on the Han"—the Han River bisecting the greater Seoul area. Interestingly, and rightfully pointed out to me after one of my lectures, most of Hyundai's operations were centered in Ulsan on the southeast coast of the peninsula.

Hyundai Group Logo

Recognized across Korea since the 1960s, the yellow and green corporate logo symbolizes stability, especially important for a company rooted in the construction industry. Drawing from the Great Pyramids of Egypt, the triangles represent mankind's long history of construction. In turn, the green and yellow reflect Korean agrarian and Confucian tradition of renewal and constant innovation akin to sprouts growing to form a green pasture.

Empire

The extended Chung family, which included Chung Ju Yung, his brothers, in-laws, children, and nephews, oversaw a considerable empire. Over time some of the brothers and brothers-in-law eventually formed their own Groups. These included the Halla Group (cement, construction, auto parts), the Sungwoo Group (cement, auto parts, accessories, batteries, resorts), Korea Flange (flanges, forging, auto parts), Hyundai Industrial Construction and Development (housing construction), Hyundai Oil Refinery, and the KCC Group (auto paint and glass). In turn these affiliated Groups provided products and services as preferred or exclusive suppliers.

These Chung family business ventures actually follow Korean norms with the eldest son (*jang ja*), in this case Hyundai, assuming responsibility for younger siblings and their families (the affiliated family owned companies). This norm still impacts business in 2014 as the Hyundai Motor Group continues to support and nurture the smaller companies.

Nation-Builder to Philanthropy

Late in life, with his family members and a loyal team of experienced managers running day-to-day operation of what had grown into a business empire, Chung Ju-yung's interests shifted from nation building to philanthropic activities. In the 1980s, his influence and determination were key to South Korea securing the 1988 Olympic Games. Moreover, Honorary Chairman Chung was among the first South Koreans to break the bonds of Cold War mentality and worked to promote economic and cultural relations with North Korea, China, and Soviet Russia.

Transition and Family Succession

Prior to Chung Ju-yung's death in 2001 and amid pressure by the government for Korea's large industrial groups to spin off unrelated divisions and focus on core businesses, the Hyundai Group restructured. In a complex re-structuring move holdings were divided among family members into several smaller Groups.

Six new Hyundai Groups emerged. Of note the eldest surviving son Chung Mong Koo assumed control over the Hyundai Motor Company with 10 auto-related affiliates, including Kia Motors, Hyundai Precision (Hyundai MOBIS), Incheon Steel (Hyundai Steel) and Hyundai Capital.

Consolidating the automotive and steel-related businesses, Chung Mong Koo became chairman of the Hyundai Motor Company. This marked a new era of leadership and direction for the carmaker. Most significant was the new HMC chairman's hands-on approach to management and issue resolution that would lead to a dramatic improvement in quality and global expansion.

Over the next ten years, some of the former Group's firms struggled to recover and ended up in receivership and were sold in the wake of the 1997 International Monetary Fund (IMF) Crisis. Interestingly, with today's solid growth of HMG and Hyundai Heavy Industries (HHI), one of the groups formed in the 2001 spin-off, some of the companies have been re-acquired. (Hyundai Autonet and Hyundai Engineering and Construction by the Hyundai Motor Group and the Hyundai Corp. by Hyundai Heavy Industries) Re-acquisition activities will probably continue in 2014 and beyond.

Chairman Chung Mong Koo

Following family expectations the third son of the elder Chung, Chung Mong Koo, joined the Hyundai Group after graduating college. By the mid 1970s he was personally involved in the launch of a new division within the Group—Hyundai Precision and Industry Company LTD. With the growth of Korea's export industry and increased transportation via ocean transport ships, Chung Mong Koo recognized the growing demand for ocean-going containers. In this new venture, Hyundai Precision's approach was to establish a standard for containers, while also gaining a competitive edge through new production technology and product development.

This quest to enter the shipping container market soon became reality. From March 1977 to August 2000 the total production of Hyundai Precision was 2.66 million TEU (Twenty-foot Equivalent Unit, a measure used for capacity in container transportation)—and 30% of the world supply. Along with Hyundai Precision's early success, Chung Mong Koo soon developed a unique culture within the greater Hyundai Group—one that strove for entrepreneurial growth and incorporated cutting edge production technology. Some milestones stand out.

110 Days

With the need to ship its own products, Hyundai Group had considered manufacturing containers since 1975. Recognizing the demand just within the Groups coupled with demand from the overall growth of the Korean export industry, Chung Mong-Koo boldly embraced the business with the conviction that timing was right to be highly successful. Once committed, construction on a container production facility began on November 10, 1976. Initially this date was known as 110—an abbreviation for the 11th month November and day 10 of the month. However, within the company 110 took on a broader, more significant meaning—the plant's construction was completed in only 110 days.

Under Construction—Hyundai Precision Manufacturing Plant. Ulsan, South Korea.

Meanwhile, as construction crews were laying foundations and erecting the building's steel girder framework, Hyundai Precision sales teams were taking orders for containers. High demand for the containers drove the team to complete the construction in record time

The Pony

Building on the successful manufacturing of shipping containers, Hyundai Precision soon looked for other expansion opportunities. With Hyundai Motor Company's launch of the *Pony*, Hyundai Precision became a supplier of automotive wheel parts. In 1986 HMC entered the North American car market with the export of the Pony II (sold as the Excel) and car parts manufacturing also became a growing business for Hyundai Precision. As demand for vehicles increased globally, so, too, did the demand for auto parts.

Early Hyundai Motor Pony

Through the eighties Hyundai Precision continued to pursue new opportunities. For example, the Asian Games and the Seoul Olympics in 1988 presented the need for locally manufactured sailing yachts. Hyundai Precision met this challenge to craft domestically built yachts for the competitions. As demand for other locally sourced and produced products surfaced, Hyundai Precision added the manufacture of golf carts, military vehicles, aircraft and even high tech rolling stock (trains).

The 1990s

In the 90s, the business strategy at Hyundai Precision shifted from labor-intensive to technology-intensive production. In addition to building upon their automotive and container business, part of this new strategy looked to the high tech machine tool business.

Under Chung Mong Koo's leadership the company laid out what would be a cutting-edge strategy to establish itself in industrial tooling. Despite its late entry into the tooling market, Hyundai Precision sought to overcome this disadvantage through a technology-based business model with (1) direct and distributor sales, (2) financial support to customers, (3) a comprehensive lease sales program, (4) a 24 hour customer and parts center, and (5) post-sales service. Success would also hinge on both domestic Korean and export sales across the Americas, Southeast Asia, and Europe, plus international quality certifications.

With the implementation of their strategy, Hyundai Precision Machine teams met the challenge—to become a high-tech business with global sales and distribution, coupled with market know-how. (Chung Mong Koo would later follow this model with Hyundai Motor Company.)

The Galloper

In addition to supporting Hyundai Motor Company as a Tier I supplier, Hyundai Precision looked to introduce its own four-wheel drive vehicle to the Korean market. In August 1988 the company developed the J-car project with a team from America's Roush Enterprises. This became X-100 ECS ROUSH. However, despite hopes the vehicle would have widespread appeal, response to the prototype by a test market study with U.S. consumers was poor. Undaunted Hyundai Precision turned to Mitsubishi for production support. A Mitsubishi model (Pajero) was selected. The Pajero would be rebranded and locally manufactured as the Galloper.

In 1991, the Hyatt Hotel in Seoul was the site of the launch for the Galloper. At the time, no one felt the Galloper could dislodge the Ssangyong Korando, the popular and dominant SUV in the Korean market. That said, it would take only a year for the Galloper to surpass the Korando.

Soon, the Galloper was a hit not only in Korea but also in Europe and Asia. This success was a result of a number of international high profile promotional and marketing activities, including the Galloper participating in long distance off road rallies—and placing well.

Record Sales

The bold Hyundai Precision sales and promotion strategy proved successful. Between 1997 and 1998

Galloper sales increased by five times. Within a broader context this success occurred during the 1997 Asian fiscal meltdown, commonly referred to as the IMF Crisis. In contrast at the same time the highly anticipated launch of the Samsung Group's automotive division in the domestic Korean market proved dismal.

Impact of the IMF Crisis

With the exception of Hyundai Precision Galloper's success in 1997 and 1998, the South Korean economy suffered greatly during the IMF Crisis. As noted earlier, amid calls by the South Korean government, the public, and global banking for wide spread reforms, the Hyundai Group and Hyundai Precision underwent substantial restructuring. For example, over the next several years, Hyundai Precision's military, railroad car and machine tool businesses would be transferred to ROTEM. This restructuring would lead to the birth of MOBIS and a vision to be a top 10 global automotive parts company.

Transformation: Prompted by the IMF, but driven by world automotive industry trends

By 1999, Chung Mong Koo had assumed control of HMC in addition to his leadership role at Hyundai Precision. Adding to his responsibilities, HMC had also acquired Kia Motors—an early casualty of the Asian financial crisis that ripped across the Korean economy. Having experience in the Hyundai Motor's after-sale service early in his career, Chung Mong Koo was not without insights into the car division. Since its founding in the mid 1970s, HMC had focused solely on growth. Indicative of Korea industry at that time, this focus was to produce as many cars as possible—as fast as possible. In turn, product quality and customer satisfaction suffered. From his experience working with consumers at Hyundai Motor's After Sales division, Chung Mong Koo knew the damage shoddy products could bring to the Hyundai reputation, not to mention the high cost of warranty repairs.

When Chung Mong Koo began sharing his intention to turn Hyundai Motor Company into a top-five automaker, few outside the company took him seriously. Hyundai, like many family-controlled Korean companies, was hierarchical and at times slow to change if there was a perceived risk. More significant, managers rarely cooperated with one another and division chiefs ran their operations as personal fiefdoms. It was a company of silos. "When a problem occurred, each division would blame other divisions," says Lee, Hyun Soon, former Hyundai-Kia Motors Vice Chairman and Chief Technology Officer. [x]

Chung Mong Koo's first step was to replace the former top management with engineers and those with whom he had worked closely at Hyundai Precision. He formulated a strategy to challenge Toyota for quality. Extensive work with a number of top global consulting firms (e.g. J.D. Powers) and benchmarking of the world's best automotive companies followed. He also sent teams to America to study weather, road conditions and driver habits. Quality control staff increased tenfold to 1,000 and they reported directly to him. Employees were encouraged to offer suggestions and were rewarded. For example, one worker reported the Sonata and XG350 Grandeur sedans had differently designed spare tire covers. Sharing a common cover saved Hyundai about $100,000.00 per year.

Chung Mong Koo quickly earned a reputation for an obsession with quality. For example, several years ago a new Sonata launch in Korea was delayed for two months with 50 issues that senior management wanted addressed. Employees in the Asan factory worked feverishly to correct these items. One was a tiny error in the size of the gap between two pieces of sheet metal near the headlight. The problem was not visible to the human eye and was narrower than 0.1 millimeter. However, numerous managers and employees worked on the problem for 25 days before it was solved. This obsession with quality continues today with the Chairman relentlessly reinforcing the quality mandate to management and teams globally as they strive for zero defects.

Turning Point

Initially, the HMC post-IMF restructuring was a combination of fiscal cuts across the company along with consolidation of duplicate services, such as R&D and parts manufacturing between the two Hyundai and Kia brands. A new marketing plan for the brands was also launched with Kia focusing on the younger and stylish consumer and Hyundai targeting an older, more mature customer. Over the next few years HMC also moved to fully integrate the core and support businesses of Hyundai Motor, Kia Motors, Hyundai Precision (renamed as MOBIS), ROTEM (also spun off from Hyundai Precision), Incheon Steel (Hyundai Steel), GLOVIS (formed in 2001 as Hankook Logitech Co. Ltd), and Hyundai Capital. This positioned HMC for a new era of growth and global success.

Concurrent with and benefitting from the restructuring, Hyundai Motor had begun production of its first SUV. Introduced for the 2001 model year, the Santa Fe became a milestone for the company. The SUV was developed during restructuring and was a huge hit with the American buyer. Marking a trend we see today, the Santa Fe was so popular that Hyundai dealers had trouble at times meeting demand.

Chapter 3

A Unique Corporate Culture, Old and New

Sahoon

Chapter 3 links the Hyundai company's heritage, culture, and values—old and new. Stepping back in Hyundai history, values were shared through the company motto or in Korean, *sa hoon.* While exact translations of the Hyundai's *sa hoon* may vary, the message is consistent. Originating with the Founder Chung Ju Yung, these are time-honored, enduring company standards and qualities of diligence, prudence and harmony.

In fact, in corporate offices of the Group in Korea and around the world, framed Korean calligraphy of the Hyundai values may be still prominently displayed. These values are a legacy well worth understanding and are strongly tied to the Hyundai Way.

Hyundai *Sahoon*

The first value is Diligence (*geun myeon*) 근면

In the workplace this translates to HARD WORK. Hyundai team members recognize that achieving worthwhile goals requires commitment, determination—and, often, long hours, especially for a company once rooted in demanding construction and engineering projects.

Next is Prudence (*geom so*) 검소

Wise and careful use of resources is a hallmark of Hyundai. Seeking maximum return with minimum investment of resources is a component of the Hyundai success model.

And finally, Harmony (*chin ae*) 친애

Teamwork, especially in times of growth and stress, requires strong collaboration and cooperation with family-like solidarity leading to success.

Complementing the *sahoon* legacy, Hyundai's core principles have great value today by driving and aligning organizational behavior. They include:

1. Innovative thinking

Within Hyundai, this means to create "something out of nothing." Hyundai has a rich heritage of entrepreneurial innovation. In action this is future-leaning innovative thinking, especially when faced with challenges.

2. Risk-taking

For Hyundai teams this means to take bold action. They seek opportunity and then take action while assuming ownership and responsibility.

3. Can Do Attitude

The company has a heritage for doing what others have said is impossible. This "Can Do" attitude means attacking challenges with 110% commitment through strong will to overcome obstacles. In Korean this is referred to as *Ha myeon dwaen da,* which translated means, "Even if it's impossible, it's still possible."

Together For A Better Future

Building upon legacy values and principles, in 2011 the Hyundai Motor Group updated the organization's management philosophy, core values and vision to meet the challenges of an ever-growing international business. They include:

1. Management Philosophy

"Realize the dreams of mankind by creating a new future through ingenious thinking and continuously challenging new frontiers."

2. Core Values

"The five core values we have defined as part of our new corporate philosophy are tenets that have existed throughout our history, and are principles that all employees promise to foster in our organization."

To better communicate the core values, icons were crafted as easily understood representations.

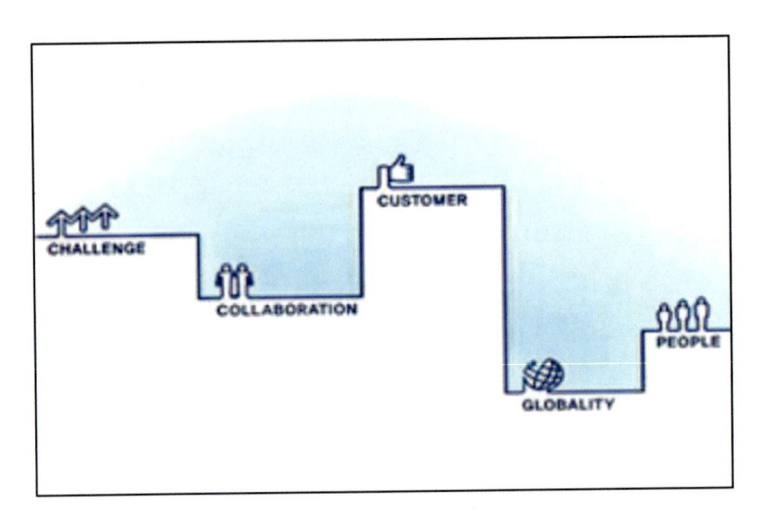

Core Value Icons

Challenge: up arrows pointing toward higher goals
Collaboration: Two people shoulder to shoulder, moving forward together
Customer: A thumbs-up representing our priority on the customer
Globality: A globe that represents our will to embrace the world
People: Individuals continually growing to reach their full potential

3. Vision

Group wide and division level vision slogans and statements were also introduced, including:
The Hyundai Group Vision Slogan: "Together for a better future"
A Group Vision Statement: "The Hyundai Motor Group aims to create ultimate value and promote harmonious growth for all stakeholders through eco-friendly management and respect for mankind."

And a specific Automotive Division Vision statement: "Lifetime partners in automobiles and beyond."

Linking the Past, Present and Future

When considering the company's founding legacies of core values and principles and the Group's new management philosophy, values and vision, we gain a deeper insight into the ever-evolving Hyundai Way. In many cases the new values and vision reaffirm the time-proven legacy values, such as "create something out of nothing," "embrace every opportunity," "achieve our goals with passion and ingenious thinking," "Move with 'Hyundai Speed'," and "Make the impossible possible with 'Can-do' thinking."

In contrast, some of the new core values, "Collaboration", for example, show how the values have been re-defined to meet the needs of a global organization.

Unlike the Korean top down management style of the past, the new value Collaboration looks to build synergy, encourage a sense of togetherness, and foster mutual communication and cooperation within the company and with business partners.

To conclude, core values and principles past and present provide a framework for better understanding HMC corporate culture. The *Hyundai Way* is a mindset as well as a way to view and execute a project or tackle a problem. Incorporating this outlook into the workday aligns teams and management to move Hyundai forward in the quest for innovation, quality, market share, and consumer satisfaction.

Chapter 4

Management Styles

Hyundai's early management style was influenced by Founder Chung Ju Yung and his charismatic personal leadership, which was also strongly tied to Korean Confucianism. Management teams of the 1960s, 1970s and 1980s, in turn, modeled their style after the Founder. In the wake of global expansion during the late 1990s and 2000s, Hyundai's management style evolved. In fact, today there are a number of methods; a few are common and the most notable autocratic and collaborative styles. All are part of what I see as Hyundai Way culture.

The Role of Mentoring

Looking back several years to a team building workshop, a senior Korean manager openly shared some insights on Korean management styles. Within his Korean division, teams were mentored by seniors in one of several styles. For example, some senior managers fostered a "soft" management style of collaboration, while others used a "hard...don't ask questions and just do it" autocratic style.

Elaborating, he explained that he was taught and preferred to first present the challenge or situation to the team and then ask the junior staff to prepare some ideas and solutions. This collaborator style was in stark contrast to a "top down" style in which communication and direction were one way. The Korean manager further noted that in the case of working in the overseas' subsidiary he found what was most effective was to ask the American colleagues for their thoughts on a matter versus directing the team's actions. He felt the former approach better tapped the experience and creativity of the local teams.

Globality

Korean teams and management have been assigned to subsidiaries worldwide and have become increasingly global savvy. This results in the teams being exposed to and embracing local management styles. Moreover, an increasing number of Korean team members have been educated at western business schools and have earned MBAs, exposing them to a broad range of leadership and management styles. At times this can also result in a generational divide between the younger managers, influenced by their western education, and the older managers and their more rigid adherence to old practices.

A Growing Trend

In my experience I see an overall growing trend toward collaboration—from top leadership to team level. There are, however, exceptions predominately because of the strong in-grained hierarchical model. For example, a Korean manager with a dominant "softer" management style may quickly shift to a more autocratic style. Typically, this is the result of a request or directive from senior leadership overriding their personal preferences in tackling a situation. In a Korean organization like Hyundai it is not appropriate for middle management and even local senior management to question or evaluate the opinions, ideas or orders of one's superiors. Leadership's role is to decide on direction and major issues. In turn, the working team's role is to implement or gather needed information. A request "from above" receives priority over other projects and scheduled meetings. If a request comes from leadership, the local Korean managers will expect all to follow and execute. In many cases, local non-Korean teams will see such a request conveyed by their Korean colleague as a one-sided demand but local teams need to recognize these hierarchical dynamics.

Finally, as a senior Korean manager once reminded me—"no two Koreans are alike," so I suggest that correspondingly no two follow identical management styles. Moreover, especially in the case of Korean expatriates working abroad, their style might shift depending on the situation as well as change over time as they are influenced and adapt.

All said, regardless of the management style, one overarching aspect of Hyundai corporate culture still dominates—once a decision is made, the expectation is that the teams move at *Hyundai Speed* to accomplish.

Conclusions

Conclusions", the final chapter in the *Hyundai Way: Hyundai Speed* series, shares my personal thoughts and opinions. I begin with the question, "Considering its strong Korean heritage and corporate culture, is the Hyundai business model globally sustainable?" I tackle this question from a cultural perspective, leaving other aspects of sustainability, such as the production network, consumer appeal and brand image staying power, for my colleagues in the automotive industry.

In my 2012 book, *Korea Facing: Secrets for Success in Korean Global Business* I note that Korean global companies as a whole have prospered and adapted well to an expanded international scope. Specifically, I call this trend *K-lobalization*.

To further define K-lobalization, I find Korean teams and management becoming increasingly global savvy. More significantly, following the global recession of 2009-10 when many international firms experienced staggering setbacks, the profits, sales and market shares of Samsung, the Hyundai Motor

Group and LG soared. As a result some Koreans consider their business model superior or at least equal to rival and established western brands.

An additional characteristic of K-lobalization is that Korean firms are boldly promoting their own unique corporate culture and management style across their global organization. This may take the form of the company-wide introduction of the corporate core values and vision, along with global training initiatives and directives. In Hyundai's case, we see this in the 2011 introduction of the new HMG management philosophy, core values, and vision (all well discussed in Chapter 3).

So, if K-lobalization is the new model, then why still hire local western leadership and management teams? Two challenges for Hyundai and other Korean multi-national Groups have been launching overseas operations and staffing the local branch or subsidiary. In part, Korean leadership is well aware that local expertise is vital for success, and, in part, no Korean Group has a sufficient Korean workforce or desire to entirely staff their international operations with expats.

Several years ago during a group session I hosted for overseas Korean and western Hyundai senior managers, the discussion turned to the "role" of the westerners in local project development. The local western Hyundai teams felt under-utilized and wanted to contribute more. This, of course, was a source of considerable frustration for the westerners because their previous employers had given them considerable responsibility with little direct oversight and fully utilized their experience and expertise.

Pondering for a moment during the discussion, a senior Hyundai Korean pointed out that local input was respected... and expected, but perhaps feedback from his side needed to be better communicated. The Korean manager went on to explain that his team knew how to do things "Korean style", but what was needed were alternate ways of approaching work related issues. Even if the local ideas were not adopted, he noted, senior management reviewed those options and took them into consideration.

In fact, on a number of occasions Korean management has shared with me that Hyundai leadership had high trust in the global organizations. They hired the local teams to provide much needed expertise and know-how.

Relevant to the Hyundai Way, the Korean team explained that the challenges and frustrations they were hearing from their western colleagues were an aspect of the company's top down "culture." Specifically, a department's role (even in Korea) was to provide support and once given an assignment to implement the project. Although perceived as restrictive to the Americans, the approach was never an attempt to limit and downplay the local teams' expertise.

Listening attentively, one of the western managers smiled and, as I recall, thanked his Korean co-worker for sharing and promised he would convey the message to his team. The western manager also commented that he wished he had understood this corporate culture dimension two years earlier, since the feedback would have reduced stress in his department. Once again *Culture* matters.

My concerns regarding sustainability

Over the years as I have worked across Hyundai as well as with other global and domestic organizations, I have come to recognize their gaps, strengths, and weaknesses. On a positive note, top management, especially at Hyundai, has increasingly becoming skilled in handling cross-cultural issues within their organizations. However, a company's success is highly dependent upon the entire team's collective grasp of the corporate culture and, in our case, the *Hyundai Way*, which I have pointed out in this book's Introduction as an intangible acquired over time.

My concern on sustainability is that few individuals can quickly develop a true understanding of Hyundai culture without training and coaching. It does not just "happen." Merely hoping the team can understand or allowing it to unfold over time is a recipe for failure and high employee turnover. Without ongoing reinforcement, even a well financed and professionally crafted Corporate Culture program will have limited impact if only offered in some form of a mandatory workshop.

I do recommend teams and key executives receive continuing "cultural" support in addition to the company's corporate training programs. In addition executives will benefit from— and appreciate— one-on-one coaching sessions that offer them an opportunity to discuss situational work-related issues privately and confidentially.

In Conclusion

With the exception of times when directives from senior leadership take priority, Korean management looks to the company's global teams and top partners for new ideas. I suggest local teams embrace the *Hyundai Way*, core culture, vision, and principles. This means moving at *Hyundai Speed* to discover innovative ways to overcome challenges, and to contribute "out of the box" thinking to accomplish "the impossible."

About the Author

Don Southerton

With a life-long interest in Korea and the rich culture of the country, Southerton has authored numerous publications with topics centering on the Korean auto industry, new urbanism, entrepreneurialism, and early U.S.-Korean business ventures. His firm, Bridging Culture Worldwide, provides strategy, consulting and training to Korea-based global business including long time support of the Hyundai Motor Group.

Credits

Hyundai Motor Group Logo, Courtesy of Hyundai Motor Group

East Asia Map, Courtesy of the author

Hyundai Group Logo, Unknown

Hyundai Pony, Courtesy of Hyundai Motor America

Hyundai Precision Under Construction, Courtesy of Hyundai MOBIS

Galloper, Courtesy of Hyundai MOBIS

Sahoon, Courtesy of the author

Hyundai Core Value Icons, Courtesy of Hyundai Motor Group

Endnotes

[i] Alfred Marshall, *Principles of Economics* 9th ed. (New York: Macmillan, 1961).

[ii] Harvey Leibenstein, T*he Collected Essays of Harvey Leibenstein*, vol. 2, Kenneth Button, ed. (Aldershot, England: Edward Elgar Publishing, 1989). Pp. 254-256.

[iii] Peter Drucker, Innovation and Entrepreneurship: Practice and Principles (New York: Harper and Row, 1985). P. 211.

[iv] World Design Capital, Seoul 2010. http://wdc2010.seoul.go.kr/eng/ Internet accessed April 16, 2011.

[v] George Gendron, "Flashes of Genius," Inc. Magazine (May 1996). An interview with Peter Drucker on entrepreneurial complacency.

[vi] Kae H. Chung, "An Overview of Korean Management," Korean Managerial Dynamics, eds. Kae H. Chung and Hak Chong Lee (New York: Praeger, 1989), p. 3. In addition and within the book, see Shim and Steers, "The Entrepreneurial Basis of Korean Enterprise: Past Accomplishments and Future

Challenges," p. 25 where the authors note that the Republic of Korea's economic success must include recognizing the national commitment by the masses to build a better nation. As for the name western scholarship and journalism most often labels the family-run conglomerates—chaebol (literally, financial cliques)—in South Korea the term has taken on a derogatory association with the financial crisis of 1997. A more acceptable term is perhaps *dae kiôp*.

[6] Chung, "An Overview of Korean Management," pp. 4-5.

[7] Ibid.

[8] Ibid.

[x] *Time*, Monday, Apr. 18, 2005 "Hyundai Revs Up," Michael Schuman

Made in the USA
Lexington, KY
18 August 2018